# STEPPING UP

## TO A LIFE OF VISION, PASSION AND AUTHENTIC POWER

## AN EXPERIENTIAL GUIDE

### AUSTIN VICKERS

# STEPPING UP

## TO A LIFE OF VISION, PASSION AND AUTHENTIC POWER

## AN EXPERIENTIAL GUIDE

### AUSTIN VICKERS

ISBN 0-9714761-2-8

**LIBRARY OF CONGRESS CONTROL NUMBER:**
2004092923

**FIRST EDITION**

Printed in the United States of America

Designed by Gerd Corrigan, www.greenteastudio.com
Photography by Phyllis Lane, www.phyllislane.net

**PUBLISHED BY QUANTUM HORIZONS BOOKS**
A Division of Quantum Horizons, LLC.

1730 E. WARNER ROAD
SUITE 10-142
TEMPE, ARIZONA 85284
480.491.5591

*"this program is gratefully dedicated to the many people who have helped me become a mentor and teacher by trusting me to be theirs."*

# TABLE OF CONTENTS

*"It is not the mountain that we conquer, but ourselves."*
*- Sir Edmund Hillary, the first man to climb Mount Everest*

Recently my son Chris decided he wanted to play for a different soccer team. He had an opportunity to step up his game to the next level, and made the commitment to try.

He has always been a pretty good soccer player. When he was very young, he would often score five or six goals, sometimes in the first half of a game. The first couple of goals he would score were always very exciting. But then it would almost get embarrassing how good he was, and how many goals he could score at will. His accomplishments on the soccer field have done a lot to feed my sports ego.

Of course, as he got older the competition increased and the difference between him and other players diminished. He was still a really good player, but he began to play on teams with other really good players, so the differences were not so obvious. Last year he found himself playing for a team that did not win as much as he would have liked, and where some of the players were not as serious about the game of soccer as he was. He was playing for a team that was the second best in his league, and he decided he wanted to "step up" his game to a new level. He decided that he wanted to try and play at the highest level, and for the best team in the league. A team that won most of its games, was ranked one of the best teams in the state, and arguably was one of the best teams in the country.

At the end of the regular season, Chris approached his coach and told him of his desire to try out for the other team in the league. His coach was supportive and encouraged him to follow his dreams, but added pressure to Chris' decision by telling him to consider some possible outcomes of that choice. For example, he told Chris that if he did not make the new team, as many other kids had not in the past, there might not be a spot for him on his team because of his need to fill roster positions. He also told Chris that even if he did make it, there would be new and more demands on his time, that he might end up sitting on the bench and not playing as much, and that there was no assurance of success with the new team. All of these possibilities were accurate, and the coach did a good job of describing for Chris the risks associated with his desire to "step up" his game, while at the same time adding some pressure to Chris to try and influence him to stay where he was.

Other players on Chris' team heard of his desire to try out for the premier team, and teased him about his decision. In typical teen fashion, they told him he was crazy to try out, and that there was no way he could make it on the new team. They tried to convince him that his skills were all in his head, and that he wasn't any better of a player than they were.

Nevertheless, and much to my delight as a father, Chris decided to go for it and give it a shot, explaining to me that he did not want to spend the rest of his life wondering whether or not he could have made it had he tried. He told me he would rather take the risk and fail, than compromise his dreams of playing with the better team. So he left his team and along with many other hopefuls from around the city, attended the tryouts for the premier team.

A few weeks later I had the opportunity to attend parent night at Chris' new high school. It was an opportunity for me, as a parent, to meet the teachers and discuss the projects and subjects that Chris would be working on through the new year. The evening took place about a week after school had begun, and already the students were working on new projects. In one class, Chris was asked to create a poster board of his life, including all of the most significant things in it. At the end of the orientation, I saw Chris' poster board for the first time, there on the wall in the classroom. It had pictures of his mother, of his sister, and of me. It told of his likes and dislikes and his passions. And it included a picture of him kicking a soccer ball during a game, a picture I thought was pretty cool.

Below the picture was a section where Chris was to describe what the most significant events of his life had been. As I read the words he had written, it was all I could do to hold back the tears in my eyes. There on the picture board was a description by Chris of how he had taken the most meaningful risk of his life to achieve his dream of playing with one of the best soccer teams in the state, and how he had achieved that dream and made the team.

It might be easy for some to diminish this experience, and to say it is only about soccer, and the achievement was not much of a feat of courage because teenage sports are not that significant. But to do so would be to fail to see the enormity of courage, vision, and passion that is enveloped in this experience. You see, it may just be a teenage soccer experience to you and I, but to Chris it was everything. He lives, eats and breathes soccer. Playing soccer is one of the most important activities of his life. Soccer was and is his world. To us, the risk may have seemed unimportant, but to Chris it represented the biggest risk of his young life. To try out for the team, and not make it, and possibly lose his spot on his current team, would be to take away a significant part of his passion, of who he is. It would have represented a failure of significant proportion - to him.

In this regard, Chris' experience is not unlike our own, in times when we too are faced with the biggest risks of our lives, and the choice of whether or not we will "step up" our game to a new level. And I believe we can learn a lot from his experience.

Stepping up requires a readiness and willingness to engage in new forms of thought, behavior and commitment required to reach a new level. It means doing something different than we are doing today to produce a different result. Like Chris' example, to step up we have to be able to imagine a different and more successful result for ourselves, as we would define it. We have to be willing to alter our behaviors and try new actions to achieve those desired results. And ultimately, we have to be so committed to reaching that new level that we are willing to assume a substantial risk of failure and the loss of something we perceive we have today.

While many people think they are ready to step up to a new level, actually doing so proves much more difficult. Stepping up inevitably takes people out of their comfort zones, requiring them to be open-minded and see things in a new way, ultimately requiring them to be accountable and responsible for their lives. It requires that they face fear head on, and be willing to step into the realm of an insecure environment that will test who they really are and what they are capable of achieving. This realm inevitably carries the potential for an interpretation that we are not as great or successful or accomplished, as our comfortable and secure environments and circumstances allow us to believe.

Many people might say they are ready to "step up" to a new level, but in truth they are quite content where they are. They prefer contentment and pleasure to growth and challenge. They might think they want different results in life and they will often tell people they do, but in truth the limiting circumstances, situations and people they maintain in their lives serve the valuable function of constructing the walls of a place that feels like home. These walls, these limitations, confirm who they really believe themselves to be. In some cases the home might not be much, but at least it feels comfortable and secure. For such people, this program will have little benefit.

However, if you have gotten to the point where you want to make a change, and you realize that you are completely accountable and responsible for the conditions and circumstances of your life, and there is no one else who can change your life but you, then I can help you. If you have arrived at that place in life where you are ready to start showing up for yourself, and you are prepared to create success in your relationships with others by taking a different approach, then this program will have great benefit for you. If you are ready and able to see how the walls of your home limit and restrict you, and how tearing these walls down can open you up to the world and to new experiences of freedom, imagination, passion and vision, then get ready for your life to change - dramatically.

*first things first*

Truth, courage and commitment are the most critical components of any successful relationship. In this program, my commitment is to help you see the "truth" of who you are, and to provide you with the structure, processes and ideas that will alter the way you perceive life, allowing you to turn any "problem" or "issue" into an opportunity and advantage. But you must make the commitment to be open-minded, to tell the truth to yourself, not in judgment, but in awareness, and to have the courage to make different choices in life, based on trust, not fear. Without this commitment on either of our parts, little will change.

If we keep our commitments to each other, however, massive changes, quantum leaps in improvement, and astonishing development are all possible through this program. Clients committed to this partnership will move forward quickly. They will find freedom, clarity and purpose instead of confusion. They will develop qualities like vision and passion that define great leaders. And they will generate enormous amounts of authentic power that can facilitate the accomplishment of any intention. But first things must come first, and to arrive at this place, we must first face and alter our illusions and our ineffective beliefs and patterns.

For most of us, it has taken many, many years to construct the illusions that impede our ability to realize our dreams. The layers go so deep that often the task of discovering ourselves, and the illusions we operate under, seems endless. Learning who we are and expanding that can indeed be a daunting task, and many give up hope or begin to compromise their dreams and passions, all the while wondering why they are so unhappy. I believe this occurs because so many people chase an elusive destination, an imagined utopia. They believe that there is somewhere they need to go, or something else they need to become to be happy, other than where and what they are in this moment. This is one of the most common illusions, but within it lies a magical paradox.

To get to where we ultimately want to go, we have to be perfectly happy not to get there, to be completely okay with where we are today. We must be "unattached" to the results that we would intend for ourselves. I know for some this may seem counter intuitive, but my experience has proven that freedom and clarity and vision and happiness ultimately come only when we let go of our attachment to their achievement. This requires patience, deep understanding and great trust. It is my objective to help you develop all three of these qualities.

Patience and trust are not easy. We want results today, and we try to create quick solutions, but the process of life is not so easily controlled. Usually, the more we live in the future and try to control the results we seek, the greater the pain and loss we experience in the present. The reason for this phenomenon is because life, real life, does not exist in the future where our expectations and attachments ultimately exist. Rather, as John Lennon once stated, "life is what is happening right now, while most people are busy making other plans."

The gifts of authentic power that we are going to develop in you through this program, gifts like passion, vision, and purpose, will come to you when you learn to live where they are found in abundance: right here, right now, in the present moment. Not in some illusionary place seeking something that is not true for you right now, or in a previous present moment that no longer is, but rather right here in this moment where life is unfolding before you. It is here that the resolution we seek is ultimately found.

So, like life itself, I too ask you to be patient and trust. Take as much time as you need to move through this program. Enjoy the process. Savor each moment that a new discovery or new awareness of yourself is made. Don't seek the dramatic moments where your life completely changes because of something you learn about yourself. Those moments will come anyway, without you having to do anything. Seek instead to discover the truth, the beauty, and the greatness of ordinary moments, of present moments, of the subtleties found in the process itself. Doing so and learning to master that ability will positively change your life in ways that, today, you cannot even imagine for yourself.

*"The first step on the path to creating vision, passion and authentic power is learning who we are. Not who we want to become, not who we sometimes pretend to be for others, not who our family or friends want us to be, and not who we think we are. But rather who we really are. After we peel away the masks, the illusions, the ego, the projections, and the perceptions of others, what is left? That is who we are at our core."*

# WHO ARE YOU?

The first step on the path to creating vision, passion and authentic power is learning who we are. Not who we want to become, not who we sometimes pretend to be for others, not who our family or friends want us to be, and not who we think we are. But rather who we really are. After we peel away the masks, the illusions, the ego, the projections, and the perceptions of others, what is left? That is who we are at our core.

Sometimes we believe that "who" is not so pretty. We are full of opinions of what is right and wrong, and good or bad, in ourselves and others. Like the judge in a courtroom, it feels powerful to sit in an elevated chair above others issuing our edicts and judgments. But negative judgment or criticism creates only a false sense of power that is sourced in the illusion that we are different than others, either not as good as they are, or somehow better. The belief in this illusion leads to criticism, blame, negative judgment, and other similar behaviors that ultimately limit our potential and our relationships with others. No one likes to spend time with someone who is being negative, critical or judgmental, and few feel a desire to support such individuals.

Ultimately we assert negative judgments or criticisms only when subconsciously we are trying to feel powerful. And the truth is, we only experience the need to feel powerful when we are lacking real, authentic power.

But there is a form of judgment that is necessary and useful and helps to create authentic power, and it is the one that manifests itself as choice: who is it that you choose to be in this moment? That is the purpose of this program, to help you see who you are today, and help you decide whether or not who you have been is who you choose to be now. To do that you must take an honest look at yourself and be willing to "see" parts of yourself that perhaps you have not wanted to see, or that you think are dark and undesirable.

Carl Jung once stated, "to show a man his shadow, is to show him his light." One cannot be without the other. This program will expose your shadow as well as your light. Exposing your darker side to the light of your awareness is important because all of the anxiety, fear, anger, or depression you experience, even though it may appear to be caused by the actions of others or external circumstances, is in reality an unconscious struggle to accept and come to terms with your own shadows and fears. Your clever ego creates complex defense mechanisms that help you believe your anxiety, fear, anger or depression is caused by others or by circumstances beyond your control. But a deeper and more truthful analysis of these emotions exposes the ego's plot to shield you from facing a deep seeded belief that is repugnant to your ego - that your shadows and fears make you weak, wrong, bad or incomplete.

As you will hopefully begin to see by moving through this program, the truth is that our shadows and fears do not make us weak, wrong, bad or incomplete - this is merely an illusion that helps keep the ego alive and feeling necessary. Rather, it is the ego's responses to our shadows and fears that create our negative emotions and the perception that we are not whole.

The way out of the captivity created by these fears and negative emotions, is not found by hiding within and behind the illusion the ego creates, but rather by exposing our shadows and fears to the light of day and discovering how these shadows and fears ultimately serve us. When we do this, we become integrated and whole, and the anger, frustration, anxiety and fear that accompany the illusion melt away - leaving us happy, peaceful, clear and powerful.

So, as you work through the exercises and questions of this first section, have the courage to be completely honest, without judgment or denial. This is the first step towards understanding how your shadows and fears ultimately help create your light and your greatness.

*life balance assessment*

On a scale of 1 to 10, with 1 being Dismal and 10 being Fantastic, rate the following areas of your life:

**Family Life**

| 1 | 2 | 3 | 4 | 5 | 6 | 7 | 8 | 9 | 10 |

**Business Life**

| 1 | 2 | 3 | 4 | 5 | 6 | 7 | 8 | 9 | 10 |

**Social Life**

| 1 | 2 | 3 | 4 | 5 | 6 | 7 | 8 | 9 | 10 |

**Spiritual Life**

| 1 | 2 | 3 | 4 | 5 | 6 | 7 | 8 | 9 | 10 |

**Financial Life**

| 1 | 2 | 3 | 4 | 5 | 6 | 7 | 8 | 9 | 10 |

**Fun Life**

| 1 | 2 | 3 | 4 | 5 | 6 | 7 | 8 | 9 | 10 |

**Personal Mission In Life**

| 1 | 2 | 3 | 4 | 5 | 6 | 7 | 8 | 9 | 10 |

**Energy Life**

| 1 | 2 | 3 | 4 | 5 | 6 | 7 | 8 | 9 | 10 |

**Physical Health**

| 1 | 2 | 3 | 4 | 5 | 6 | 7 | 8 | 9 | 10 |

*important questions*

Do you tell the precise truth 100% of the time to anyone and everyone who asks you a question?
___ yes ___no.  If no, why not?

_____

_____

_____

_____

_____

Would you be able to disclose to anyone  - anything and everything that you have ever done in your life,
or that has ever happened to you?  ___ yes ___ no.  If no, why not?

_____

_____

_____

_____

_____

How and to whom are you being dishonest in your life?  Please list every area.

_____

_____

_____

_____

What don't you want others to know about you?

_____

_____

_____

_____

What part(s) of you do you feel must be kept from other people, or a particular person, in order for you to feel safe?

_____

_____

_____

_____

_____

Can you think of someone, who is similar to you in the ways that you have kept hidden about yourself, but who has been truthful and public about those parts of themselves and are happy and successful anyway? ____ yes ____no. If yes, why do you think they are happy and successful anyway despite the disclosure?

_____

_____

_____

_____

_____

Do you see the role that judgment plays in your inability to disclose, or your discomfort in disclosing, to others any part(s) of your life? ___yes ___no. If yes, describe.

_____

_____

_____

_____

_____

How would you feel and who would you be, if you could disclose to everyone and anyone everything that you are, and everything that you have ever done, with complete honesty and without judgment?

_____

_____

_____

_____

_____

Do you ever get angry, upset or saddened? ___ yes ___ no. Describe one person, place or thing that consistently makes you angry, upset or saddened?

_____

_____

_____

_____

_____

Do you know anyone who does not get angry, upset or saddened in the same way you do in reaction to that person, place or thing? ___yes ___no. If yes, what do you think is the difference between you and them?

_____

_____

_____

_____

_____

In what ways do you act, or what circumstances do you create, that are like the person or circumstance that angers, saddens or upsets you? Describe.

_____

_____

_____

_____

_____

How would your life be different if you could see people or circumstances that normally anger, upset or sadden you in a different way, a way that did not bother you?

_____

_____

_____

_____

_____

How happy are you on a scale of 1 - 10: ___. If less than 10, what would you need in your life to be a ten?

_____

_____

_____

_____

_____

Do you know anyone in life who does not have the thing that you believe you need, but are totally happy anyway? ___yes ___no. If yes, what do you believe is the difference between them and you?

_____

_____

_____

_____

_____

Have you ever not had that thing in your life, but yet have been totally happy anyway? ___yes ___no. If yes, describe why you were happy and what is the difference between then and now.

_____

_____

_____

_____

_____

How would it make you feel if you knew that you did not need anything more than what you have right now in your life to be totally happy?

_____

_____

_____

_____

_____

If you were single, had twenty million dollars in the bank, and could have any partner that you desired, would you date your present partner? ___ yes ___ no. If no, why not?

_____

_____

_____

_____

_____

If no, why do you stay with your present partner?

_____

_____

_____

_____

_____

Do you believe the person of your dreams would want to be with you while you are, and so long as you choose to be, with someone you are not passionate about and happy with? ___yes ___no.

_____

_____

_____

_____

_____

What kind of person would you be if you did not accept less than what you really want and you chose only to spend time with people and things you were really passionate about?

_____

_____

_____

_____

_____

To be happy with someone in your life who consistently makes you unhappy, how would you need them to change?

_____

_____

_____

_____

_____

Who would you be and how would you feel if you did not need them to change in order to be happy?

_____

_____

_____

_____

_____

Has anyone in your life every accused you of being the same way that they are? ___yes ___no. If yes, who and when?

_____

_____

_____

_____

_____

In what ways can you see yourself in them?

_____

_____

_____

_____

_____

What is your greatest fear?

_____

_____

_____

_____

In all the years of your life, has your greatest fear ever been realized or come to pass?  ___yes ___no.

If you took all of the time and energy you have ever spent thinking about or feeling that fear, and spent all of it following your passions and your dreams, how do you think your life would be different today?

_____

_____

_____

_____

_____

What could you do to release your fear(s)?

_____

_____

_____

_____

_____

If you had twenty million dollars in your bank account, would you continue in your present job or vocation?___yes___no.  If no, why not?

_____

_____

_____

_____

_____

Do you have a plan in place for, and are you working towards, following your passions in life? ___yes ___no. If no, why not and if so, how?

_____

_____

_____

_____

_____

List the three characteristics of life that you desire most (e.g., peace, love, security, wisdom, excitement, etc.)

_____

_____

_____

_____

_____

How would your friends, family, and peers describe you?

_____

_____

_____

_____

_____

How do you define success?

_____

_____

_____

_____

_____

What about success is important to you?

_____

_____

_____

_____

_____

_____

_____

In what areas has your success been limited?

_____

_____

_____

_____

What are your business, health, family, primary relationship and emotional well-being goals for this year?

_____

_____

_____

_____

What is possible for you if you had no limits?

_____

_____

_____

_____

_____

What will bring you freedom from every limitation you have created for yourself?

_____

_____

_____

_____

_____

What are the highest priorities in your life?

_____

_____

_____

_____

_____

What are your thoughts consistently focused on?

_____

_____

_____

_____

_____

What questions do you consistently ask yourself?

_____

_____

_____

_____

_____

What does your thinking look like to others?

_____

_____

_____

_____

_____

What are you putting up with?

_____

_____

_____

_____

_____

What is life asking you to do differently?

_____

_____

_____

_____

_____

What is it you want that you haven't already achieved?

_____

_____

_____

_____

_____

If you were brave, what would you do?

_____

_____

_____

_____

_____

What will your legacy be?

_____

_____

_____

_____

_____

Do you have a mission for your life? If yes, describe it.

_____

_____

_____

_____

_____

If you were guaranteed success with no possibility of failure, what would you be doing?

_____

_____

_____

_____

_____

What is the most profound way that failure has helped you gain an edge?

_____

_____

_____

_____

_____

Is your lifestyle, the lifestyle you envisioned for your life?  If so please describe why.  If not, describe your ideal lifestyle.

_____

_____

_____

_____

_____

What would create ultimate happiness for you?

_____

_____

_____

_____

_____

What has been your greatest contribution to society?

_____

_____

_____

_____

_____

Who have been your greatest teachers throughout your life and what have been the most significant principals that you have learned from these teachers?

_____

_____

_____

_____

_____

What are the characteristics you like best about yourself and the traits that you would most like to change, develop or improve?

_____

_____

_____

_____

_____

How could you best create a way for you to consciously connect with your wise self on a daily basis?

_____

_____

_____

_____

_____

What personal issues or challenges are repeatedly blocking your success?

_____

_____

_____

_____

_____

Do you consistently keep your commitments with yourself? If not, what has to happen for you to consistently keep commitments to yourself?

_____

_____

_____

_____

_____

What actions could you do, that you are currently not doing, that if put into place on a regular basis would make a tremendous difference in your life? List one or more actions for the following areas: business, friendship, family, emotional well-being, and primary relationship.

_____

_____

_____

_____

_____

Who have you harmed or who has harmed you that you would like to release the feeling around forever?

_____

_____

_____

_____

If you had any regrets, what would they be and what can you do to release the feelings around them forever?

_____

_____

_____

_____

_____

If you have any resentments, who or what do you resent?  (Start with yourself, then family, friends, relationships, and business associates)

_____

_____

_____

_____

_____

What are you willing to do or face up to, so that the feelings around the resentments are released forever?

_____

_____

_____

_____

_____

What are you willing to give or give up to have an extraordinary life in all areas?

_____

_____

_____

_____

_____

What good do you believe will come into your life as a result of this program?

_____

_____

_____

_____

_____

Who do you really believe you are?

_____

_____

_____

_____

_____

_____

_____

_____

_____

_____

_____

_____

_____

_____

_____

_____

_____

_____

_____

_____

_____

_____

_____

_____

_____

_____

_____

_____

_____

_____

_____

**WRITE DOWN YOUR TRIUMPHS, BREAKTHROUGHS, AND TURNING POINTS**

**DATE    SPECIFICALLY, WHAT HAPPENED**

_____    _____

_____    _____

_____    _____

_____    _____

_____    _____

_____    _____

_____    _____

_____    _____

_____    _____

_____    _____

_____    _____

_____    _____

_____    _____

_____    _____

_____    _____

_____    _____

_____    _____

_____    _____

_____    _____

_____    _____

_____    _____

_____    _____

# "You are what you love, not what loves you."

Y ou will find there is a direct correlation between our state of happiness and passion and the degree to which we are spending our time with those people, places and things to which we are really attracted. This exercise is designed to help you identify where you are spending your time and how authentic you are being with yourself. In the spaces provided, list the people, places and things to which you are attracted, and the people, places and things in your life to which you feel obligated. In some cases a particular person, place or thing may be on both sides. The degree to which you are following your passions and attractions, and spending your life doing that which you love, and not that which simply loves you or to which you feel obligated, will undoubtedly be the degree to which you are really happy in life. To begin to create greater happiness in your life, move your time, attention and focus to the people, places and things to which you are attracted.

|  | ATTRACTIONS | OBLIGATIONS |
|---|---|---|
| **PEOPLE** | _____ | _____ |
|  | _____ | _____ |
|  | _____ | _____ |
|  | _____ | _____ |
|  | _____ | _____ |
| **PLACES** | _____ | _____ |
|  | _____ | _____ |
|  | _____ | _____ |
|  | _____ | _____ |
| **THINGS** | _____ | _____ |
|  | _____ | _____ |
|  | _____ | _____ |
|  | _____ | _____ |
|  | _____ | _____ |

*"Stepping up requires a readiness and willingness to engage in new forms of thought, behavior and commitment required to reach a new level. It means doing something different than we are doing today to produce a different result. We have to be willing to alter our behaviors and try new actions to achieve those desired results. And ultimately, we have to be so committed to reaching that new level that we are willing to assume a substantial risk of failure and the loss of something we perceive we have today."*

# WHO DO YOU CHOOSE TO BE NOW?

Hopefully, you have learned a lot about yourself in answering the questions outlined in the first section. Undoubtedly, you discovered areas where you are not living honestly and true to yourself, and where you are compromising your own dreams and passions. These are the places for you to do your work. These are the areas where you can evaluate whether or not your old patterns, habits and choices really serve you, or whether they are based in fears and illusions that have never really been true for you anyway.

For example, a common fear many people have is over money and finances. You would not believe the number of people I meet who spend an enormous amount of their time worrying about their finances or about money, and who do not follow their real passions in life because they believe they cannot make enough money doing it. So they compromise their dreams because of the fear and end up living lives of compromise and unhappiness.

When I work with such individuals I always ask them the same question. "Since the day you were born on this planet, when have you ever not had enough money?" Occasionally I will get someone who tries to describe for me some hardship they have endured because they did not have enough, but all end up admitting to me eventually that ultimately they have always had at least enough money or financial help to survive.

This is a typical example of the power of illusions. Despite forty or fifty years of evidence that they will be okay and they will always have enough money or financial support to survive, many people still spend much of their present moment time and energy compromising their passions and desires, worrying about money and the future, and living in fear. Why?

Because they have not taken the time to deeply examine those fears and discover the illusions that create them, and they do not have much experience following their passions and desires despite their fears. Living in, and acting out of, fear to one extent or another has become comfortable and habitual for them, and much easier than the courage and effort it takes to follow their hearts and passions and not allow fear to control their lives.

I want to be clear here. I am not judging the choice to live or act in fear as bad or wrong. The truth is we all experience fear, and we all have allowed fear to govern or dictate our choices, to one extent or another at different times in our lives. Philosophically, I believe that there is a soulful purpose for fear in our lives and when we act in fear we are satisfying some deeper aspect of our souls that needs to be satisfied in that way, at that time.

But if you are reading this book and are choosing to embark on this program, then it is likely that you have decided you want a different experience. At some deeper level you intuitively understand that to create different results in life, you need to see things differently and make different choices. And you have probably decided that you want less fear in your life, and you want to follow your heart and live a life more full of passion, vision, and authentic power.

This section outlines a way for achieving that life. On each page there is a principle, an application idea, and a section to journal your experience with the principle and its application to your life. Make it a point to read one a week, and work on the application of that principle during the week. Then, when the week is over, write down your experiences. Really working with these principles and exercises in your daily life, and recording and reflecting on your experiences, will transform who you are. I know this because they have transformed my life and the lives of countless others who have taken the time to seriously consider the most important question you will ever answer.

*"who do you choose to be now?"*

# PASSIONATE

*"follow your heart and let the flame of your passion and enthusiasm burn bright, so all may see and feel the warmth of the light that you offer."*

Application Idea: To become passionate about life, you just have to follow your passions. Does that sound overly simplistic? If it does, it is because it is that simple. Yet very few of us fully follow our passions. That is because we have difficulty trusting that, if we follow our passions, instead of what we think we "should do," everything will be okay. So we come up with excuses instead: "It's not very practical" or "what would my family think" or "I don't have enough money to take that risk" or "I may not find something better." We feel fear about embracing what we are really passionate about, and so we compromise. And we do things, and stay with people we are not passionate about, and then we wonder why we do not feel passionate or excited or happy about life. Identify one thing in life that you would be really passionate about, but you are not currently doing. Perhaps it is a hobby, or be involved with a person you really respect, or tackling a new project like building something, writing a book, or learning a new language or instrument. Then, make it a point today to begin adding this passion to your life. Learn about it, create an opportunity for it to be in your life, and then live it. If you do, you will start to notice the flames of your passion growing hotter and brighter.

*"the body not only grows tired of physical activity, but also tires of pursuing that which does not satisfy our passion and purpose."*

Application Idea: We have obligations to ourselves to pursue the dreams and desires of our hearts, and when we do so, the body responds positively. When we are pursuing our passions, we no longer need the amount of rest that our bodies demand while doing other things that do not feed our passion or advance our purpose in life. You can observe this simply by paying attention to how your body feels when you are engaging in your favorite hobby or pastime, and then comparing that to how you feel following your day to day routine. Undoubtedly, you will notice a difference in your energy levels. Today, try to engage in an activity that really inspires you. Take up a new hobby or activity you have been thinking about for some time. Or begin writing that book or song, or painting that picture that has been hanging around in your mind. Or pick up a sport or activity that you no longer do, that used to bring you a lot of happiness when you were younger. Write about the feelings, emotions and energy you experience while engaged in this activity. Feeding your passion will help it to grow within you.

*"purpose of being can never be attained without the willingness to define and stand for what you believe."*

Application Idea: Having a purpose and a focus in life that we are passionate about is essential to our well-being and happiness. It is like the rudder of a prized racing yacht that helps steer the racing vessel quickly and efficiently to its desired destination. Without the rudder, the yacht may be capable of moving quickly, but it will have difficulty going anywhere or staying on course. Likewise, without a sense of purpose we may be capable of great things, but we will have difficulty achieving them. To regain a sense of purpose and passion, it is necessary to first be in touch with who you are, what you stand for, and what you believe. Make a list of the top ten beliefs or principles that you believe in. Write down these beliefs or principles, giving time and attention to each word, each sentence, so that they truly represent what you believe and can be passionate about. As you write them down, make a note also of how it feels to give definition to your principles, values and beliefs. Finally, as you evaluate the purpose and direction of your life, compare possible paths against these values and principles. The extent to which a potential path or purpose correlates to the list of your beliefs and values, is the extent to which you will feel fulfilled and happy.

> *"love is our essence and when we allow it to shine within and from us, we become consumed in love's fire."*

Application Idea: Love is the very essence of peace, happiness and satisfaction. Indeed, it is the inspiration behind these things. When we experience peace, happiness or satisfaction, we are enveloping ourselves for that brief moment in the essence of love. When we desire and the desire is fulfilled, the moment of satisfaction is the moment that love reigns freely and is allowed to envelop our very being. We often do not allow such moments to last and our egos and insecurities quickly return us to new desires. But the moment of fulfillment is when we come face to face with love and there is nothing between it and us. The path to finding lasting peace and happiness in our lives, is to find these moments of peace, happiness and satisfaction in ordinary events. This requires that you take a closer and deeper look at the present moment than you are perhaps used to doing. If you are like most people, many of your thoughts are spent thinking about the past or the future. But, as you know, you can't change the past, and the future is speculative. Time spent in either of these places, therefore, robs you of the ability to fully appreciate what is happening right now. And right now is where the beauty of life is unfolding. Make it a point to bring your awareness to the present moment. Make a note of everything in your life that is going right, and the relationships that are meaningful to you and that are bringing value to your life. Identify and write down everything going on this moment that brings joy to your life. This is an exercise of appreciation, the very act of which will bring you a closer association to love, peace and happiness.

*"the true path to happiness, passion and vision is found by following your own heart and doing so even though others do not follow or even understand your direction."*

Application Idea: We are all attracted to different ideas, people, places and things, and it is because of these differences that we are able to create for ourselves a distinct identity, that we are able to define who we are. The variety of life creates the construction materials from which we get to build ourselves. This is the path of our heart and soul. As Ralph Waldo Emerson once noted, following our attractions in life is the best way to follow our hearts, for the intention of the heart manifests itself through our attractions. An important step towards living a life of vision, passion and authentic power is identifying and following your attractions. Write down any activity or choice that you have thought about making, and that you are attracted to making, but as of yet have not been able to do. Write down the steps you would take if you were going to actively pursue that activity or choice in your life. Then simply make a decision today, to step up, follow your heart and do it, step by step, from the start, right here, right now. Doing so will dramatically change your life.

*"who do you choose to be now?"*

# VISIONARY

*"do not fear new or different teachings or beliefs. be open to the possibility that they may have more relative truth for you today than do your existing beliefs and values. try to assess them from a position of whether and how they can positively affect your life and the lives of others, rather than from a point of comparison to your existing beliefs."*

Application Idea: stretch yourself to get involved in a discussion with someone from a different political, social, religious or cultural perspective than your own. Rather than talking too much and engaging them with your beliefs, however, try to simply ask questions and listen to their point of view, taking the time to deeply explore their perspective and the reasons why they believe the way they do. Pay particular attention to those beliefs or views that cause you the most negative emotion, or that make you feel the most emotionally reactive or charged. These are the areas where you are most blocked, and where you have the most potential for growth. Ask questions to understand, not to dispute or prove wrong their point of view. Increasing your understanding of others and finding that which is common between you will help you build and establish more diverse relationships and a stronger network of support.

*"learn to become a master of yourself and to view negative circumstances and people as teachers who can show you ways to improve and empower yourself. strive to choose loving and peaceful reactions to every situation and person that challenges you, and your internal power will grow infinitely."*

Application Idea: Try to become a master of yourself in at least one situation that causes you anger, upset, anxiety, frustration, or any other kind of negative emotion. Rather than react to the person who triggers these emotions in you, try to stop and identify the reason within you that is causing the upset. Has the person showed you a part of yourself you do not like? Have they triggered in you a tendency to be controlling, and prevented you from getting the result you desired? Have they exposed a part of you that you believe to be a weakness? Ask yourself whether or not you have ever acted like they are acting. For certain they are teaching you something about yourself that is difficult for you to see - that is why you want to transfer this emotion to an external cause, rather than own it as your own. Find the reality of the situation by keeping your focus on yourself when you get upset, rather than others. Once you have identified your own role and issue in the situation, thank the negative circumstance or person in your heart for showing you a part of yourself you have not seen before.

*"we assume our ability to think is a product of the mind within our bodies. but, perhaps, intelligence that can think is the energy that learned to create that which we call mind and body."*

Application Idea: The real power of life is unleashed not through external learning, but rather through internal understanding, awareness and connection to the intelligence responsible for our creation. One begins to grow in knowledge and understanding when one ventures within, instead of constantly seeking without. Put yourself in a quiet place where your can relax your body and be free from outside distractions. As you begin to relax, focus on your breathing until it becomes rhythmic and deep. Once you are relaxed, picture yourself going deep inside your body, and imagine a room within that can only be accessed by you. Inside the room, see flowers and plants and objects that you love. Then, imagine someone entering the room. This someone is a deeper part of your self. They can be whomever they show up to be. Have a conversation with them, asking them anything about yourself that you wish to know. Be patient with their response, and do not try to impose your own desired responses on them. Rather, wait for them to respond to you with their wisdom and thoughts. You may be quiet surprised at what they have to say to you. Once you finish the conversation, thank them for their advice and come back out of your state of meditation. The whole experience should last less than a half an hour. The response and advice that you will receive comes from the intelligence that is responsible for your very being. Trust it.

*"we cannot fairly judge our own circumstances, for we do not know where they will ultimately lead. what may appear today to be a failure cannot be declared one until its outcome is final, for it may in fact lead to even greater success."*

Application Idea: I want you to think of a time when you believed something bad was happening, but it ultimately turned out to be something really good in your life. Perhaps it was the loss of a job, the loss of a relationship, or some other similar type event that ultimately opened new doors for you. Write the experience down, and reflect on how your initial judgment about the event was premature and shortsighted. Now think of a situation in your life today that is causing you pain, anxiety, upset or fear. Try to evaluate the negative judgments you are making about the situation and notice how many of your negative thoughts about it are based on speculation, hypothetical what-ifs, and illusion. Consider possible outcomes from the situation that are likely to result from having a negative or positive perspective. Resolve to have the positive consequences be the outcome of the situation you are facing today.

*"in the end, our bodies are merely specific physical manifestations of the energy that exists in all life."*

Application Idea: We think of our bodies, minds and souls as being distinct and separate, but they are not. The energy that circulates in our bodies is the same energy that flows through all life. It is the same energy that we use to formulate or receive thoughts and initiate action. It is also the energy that is responsible for the creation of life. This energy is the web that connects all life and that forms our connection with each other and all things. You can start to become aware of these patterns of energy by noticing your own energy and how it can affect the energy of people around you. One of the things I like to do when I am in the presence of what feels like negative energy, is to see if I can energize the situation with my thoughts and intentions. If someone is being negative with me, I will think and intend patterns of loving energy to surround them and embrace them and help them to overcome their experience of fear. Then I try to notice if my sending them positive, harmonious energy has any effect on their state of being. Often it does in a very tangible way. Take some time to experiment with your own ability to alter the energy patterns and vibrations of people and circumstances around you, and document your experience.

*"being open-minded means that we acknowledge we are placing our interpretation on everything, seeing everything from only one point of space and time, one point of view. it also means we acknowledge that there are endless different points from which to view any thing and every thing, any one of which would necessarily change the appearance or interpretation of that thing."*

Application Idea: One of the first facts that you must learn to accept if you really want to make significant changes in your life, is that your truth is not the truth. It is simply a story, among many, that you have chosen to see. So long as you believe that your truth is the absolute truth, your growth will be limited. The minute you recognize, however, that it is simply a story and that you can choose to see a different story or interpretation of the facts of your life, then you become prepared to have your life change in some very significant ways. I want you to reconsider a story of your life that over the years has caused you pain, suffering or fear. Perhaps someone did something to you, offended you, or hurt you in some way. Or they did not take actions you believed they should have to care for you and love you. Whatever it is, I want you to examine your story about it. Then ask yourself this question: what other interpretation could you give to the facts? Can you think of an interpretation that is more loving and that does not include the malice you have attributed to the other players involved? Can you think of an alternative explanation that allows you to benefit from the pain, rather than be hurt by it? Can you think of how your fear may have contributed to the situation in a negative way, and how reacting in a non-fearful way might help resolve the negative feelings and emotions associated with the situation? As you evaluate such an alternative, consider how it would change things if you knew that you alone were responsible for the outcome of that situation or circumstance.

*"non-attachment does not mean getting rid of physical possessions. getting rid of attachment is a process of the mind. the link that forms the "mine" of our existence is within, not without. if we rid ourselves of this link, then we become unattached and we rid ourselves of misery."*

Application Idea: To become truly happy and balanced in life, we must be willing to let go of our control and attachment to results. Often I hear people question the principle of non-attachment, believing that we should set goals and be attached to their achievement. There is, however, an important distinction to make. It is a good habit to plan, set goals, and initiate action. All of these attributes help us to accomplish and create the life that we want. Non-attachment does not mean not planning, not acting or not setting goals. Non-attachment means letting go of necessarily achieving the intended results. If life turns out differently than the path you have planned, try to find opportunity in the different results and assume that life is delivering you an outcome that is greater than anything you could have ever dreamed of for yourself. Consider and write down something in your life that is not unfolding as you expected. Rather than spending time contemplating how you might change the outcome to match your original expectations, try and consider other possible outcomes that might result from the way it is unfolding that would be of greater benefit to your life than the outcome you originally expected. Write down at least five ways that other unintended results could benefit your life. Learning to perceive in this way will allow you to see value in the change, be more flexible and open-minded, and will facilitate more effectively your ability to respond positively and opportunistically to changes in your life.

*"to be or not to be are equal parts of being."*

Application Idea:  You might as well get used to life not always presenting circumstances or people that flow smoothly for you.  Our challenges and so-called failures are an extremely important part of life. Without them, we would have no appreciation for our growth and we would learn nothing about ourselves.  So life grants us fullness, and in addition to the grace and flow it creates, it also creates situations and circumstances that challenge us and force us to look inward and evaluate who we really are.  The response that all truly successful and happy people employ in life is to turn these challenges into opportunities.  This is a function of attitude and perception only.  Challenge yourself to see negative circumstances, situations or people in your life in a new way.  What can you learn from the situation, circumstance or person, and how can you convert the issue or problem into an advantage.  This requires focus, not on the problem itself, but on the solution or the way out of the problem.  Write down every person and situation in life that you are finding to be challenging and problematic.  Try to see the opportunity that the circumstance or person may be manifesting for you by creating a situation that is not flowing.  Write down the values that these challenging situations or people are providing you.  Finally, make a note of whether your willingness to see these negative circumstances or people in your life in a new way creates a different effect on your state of peace and happiness.  I guarantee that it will.

*"we cannot feel unhappy when we are feeling and expressing gratitude, because gratitude to unhappiness is like light to darkness. in the presence of one, the other cannot exist."*

Application Idea: More often than not, when someone is feeling unhappy with their life it is because they have lost perspective and have a distorted view of the context of their lives. They have lost focus on what is of value in their life, and instead have developed a myopic view of their problems and challenges. In essence, they have become self-absorbed. One of the reasons people get so much value in doing charitable work or in giving service to others is because, in addition to feeling good about themselves for helping others, they also gain context and perspective about their own life. Nothing will make you appreciate your life faster than experiencing the problems and issues that other people face. Instant gratitude. If you are not doing so already, identify a charitable cause or service organization to which you could donate some of your time. Contact them and set up a meeting to offer your time on a weekly basis, even if it is just an hour or two. Try to pick an organization and an activity that will allow you personal contact with the people who will receive benefit from your actions. Seeing and experiencing the lives of others less fortunate than you will have a profound effect upon your vision and perception of life, and will allow you to live more fully in gratitude and appreciation. Whatever you are capable of giving will be nothing in comparison with what you will receive from this experience.

*"take it upon yourself from this moment onward to always look for and focus upon the magic in life, and do not accept limitations to your dreams. to accomplish great things, we must not only act, but also dream, not only plan, but also believe. our dreams and our beliefs define the upper limits of what we can achieve."*

Application Idea: How much time do you spend dreaming and thinking out of the box? In our hurry-up culture, dreaming and looking for magical moments often gets criticized as being lazy, unproductive or unrealistic. Could you imagine how most people would react in a typical corporation if, when asked what they were doing in their office staring out the window, they responded by saying they were dreaming? In many places they might get fired. Yet dreaming should not be reserved for poets, inventors and writers. Dreaming is a necessary part of all of our lives and must be nurtured, honored and encouraged within us if we are to step outside of our limitations and expand into new horizons. Identify an area of your life - work, finances, relationships, health, or your own personal well-being - that you would like to improve or achieve greater results. Then commit yourself to thinking up twenty new ideas for improvement in that area. The first ten should be intentionally outrageous and be ones that you believe have little chance of ever working or being implemented. Be outrageous and wild with your ideas and do not qualify them before putting them down on paper. The idea here is to practice getting out of your comfort zone. After you have finished putting down your wild ideas, then try to think up ten ideas you believe may have a chance of working. Write down your ideas and make it a point to revisit the list a couple of days later. Whenever you are feeling uninspired, engage this exercise to get your mind expanded out of your comfort zone and your limited thinking.

*"who do you choose to be now?"*

# AWARE

*"to have a healthy body we must learn to appreciate that which the body has to offer. we learn this appreciation first through awareness, and then by engagement."*

Application Idea:  Become aware of your senses by focusing your attention on them whenever and wherever you can. By simply taking time each day, or ideally in each moment, to focus upon that which you are experiencing, you will more fully engage your senses.  As you do so, you honor and appreciate your body.  As you honor and appreciate your body, so too will your body honor you, by giving you more of that which you are appreciating.  Your senses will come alive and your life will become filled with the richness and glory of your existence.  Stop and notice what each one of your senses (sight, sound, smell, taste, touch or feel) is experiencing right now.  Try to hold your focus on each sense for at least a couple of minutes, and go deep with the information that each of your senses is providing.  As you focus on each sense, try to imagine it becoming more acute, and offer your appreciation to it for what it has offered you in that moment. Record your experience and the feelings that it produces.

*"all living things have vibration and energy and between living things this energy and life is shared. it is how we communicate at a level beyond our physical senses. in nature we become energized, active and alert because we absorb so much of the energy and life that exists there."*

Application Idea: When we engross ourselves in nature, we become synchronized to the natural rhythms of life and energy that exist there and our bodies respond positively as they become enriched with the energy that is the source of all life. Make it a point to enjoy some aspect of nature that is around you. Take a walk in the park, go down by the lake or ocean or river, or go hiking in the mountains or hills around you. While you are in the environment, find and observe one aspect of nature that you have not paid attention to before. Write about this observation and try to find within it a metaphor for your own life, and some aspect of it that you are currently experiencing.

## *"music is the rhythm of body, mind and spirit."*

Application Idea: Music is nothing but a pattern of changing vibrations. The string on the guitar when struck resonates and vibrates to create a particular sound. A piano makes sounds when a soft mallet strikes a piano's strings, causing them to vibrate. These vibrations are then organized into patterns, which become songs. Music is the result. In sum, music is simply a changing pattern of vibration. Quantum physicists tell us we are also a changing pattern of vibration. We also know that the energy or vibration of music interacts with our energy. Depending upon the kind of music we listen to, we either create harmony or disharmony between the energy of the music we are listening to and that which forms our bodies. When the energy of music resonates with the energy within us, harmony is created and positive feelings and emotions result. When the vibration of the music conflicts with our own vibrations, disharmony is created and anxiety and stress can result. Collect and organize the music that most inspires you. Find the music that you used to listen to as a child or teenager. Collect your favorite musical scores from movies. Create a section in your musical library that you can turn to whenever you need to be inspired. Begin and end the day listening to this music, and let the notes and sounds of music resonate with the very essence of your being. Record how listening to this music, to each song, makes you feel energetically.

*"past memories and future concerns should not be permitted to cloud the sunshine that is emitted from present moments. every moment of your existence is an opportunity for you to enjoy, appreciate, and love the life that is unfolding before you."*

Application Idea: The first time you begin to feel fear, anxiety, concern, pain, or any other negative emotion, stop and take notice where you are in time. Are you in the present moment, focusing on what is happening right now? Or are you thinking about something that you think may happen, or that has already happened? Undoubtedly, it is either a past or future concern that is causing you stress, because fear exists in the past and future and not in the present moment. Any time spent in the past or future is time that could be spent focusing upon the beauty of the present moment. A great exercise for becoming present is to stop and take ten or fifteen minutes to focus on each one of your senses. Try to find something that you can see, hear, smell, taste, touch and feel that is enjoyable and pleasurable, wherever you are. Devote a couple of minutes to each sense, trying to find more subtle pleasures than perhaps you have noticed before. Try to look beyond the obvious. As you do this, not only will you become more present moment focused, but you will also develop the acuity of your senses. Write down what you see and how the experience makes you feel.

*"not only does our state of being affect our breathing, but so too does our breathing help create our state of our being."*

Application Idea: Long, slow, deep breathing contributes to a state of awareness and acute perception. That is why all meditation begins with a focus on our state of breathing. But we should not be concerned with our breathing only during meditation. We can benefit from a focus on breathing properly throughout the day. Consequently, become aware of the state of your breathing at all times. Make it a point at least five times a day to slow your breathing down and practice taking long, deep breathes that fill your lungs completely. At least once a day, practice this form of breathing with your eyes closed, sitting upright, and doing your best to clear your mind of any thoughts or activities. Record how the change in breathing changes your feelings or emotions. A more intentional focus on deep breathing will help create a body and mind that is balanced and calm, and open to imagination, creativity and inspiration.

*"when we become present moment focused and aware of all of our senses, we begin to have a new appreciation for life. we become less dependent upon distractions and we become more aware of the value of what is happening now, in this moment. as we do, the beauty and grace of life fills our consciousness and we lose sight of our problems and our fears."*

Application Idea: Take a moment right now to notice what is going on around you. Pay particular attention to detail, spending more time looking at the objects you see every day with greater perception, focus and observation. Try to find more beauty in things you may often take for granted. For example, notice that the sky is not just the sky, but rather it is a collection of muted and blended colors and shapes that cast shadows and highlights everywhere. Notice that it is a bastion of different smells that comes to us via the breeze, and how it creates a sensation of warmth or cold that we can feel on our skin. Notice the plants and trees and how they dance and play in the wind, and create playgrounds for all kinds of life. Smell their fresh fragrances, feel their varied textures, and see the intricacies of their patterns and shapes. The world is a collection of wonders, much of which we fail to see. But this wonder and beauty can return to us by a readjustment of our awareness. By simply paying attention to that which we have previously ignored, we can rediscover life and in so doing, rediscover ourselves. Identify with each one of your senses something you have not noticed before, and record this awareness and the feelings that the experience generates within you.

*"feed your body with live foods, replenish it with plenty of fresh clean water, supplement it with vitamins and minerals, and use plants and live foods liberally. if you follow these simple rules, your physical garden will flourish."*

Application Idea: Often many of us eat and drink unconsciously. The foods and drinks we choose are more often the consequence of habit, rather than the consequence of conscious choice. The good news here is that habits can be changed, and so can food and drink preferences. To do so, one simply has to begin to change the conditions that lead to the formation of the habit, and begin to create different associations and perceptions to the foods and drinks we consume. Begin to make small changes to your diet. Replace half of your coffee, tea or soda intake with clean water, and make it a point to read articles about the negative health affects of stimulants. Begin to eat more live foods, replacing processed snacks with your favorite fruits and vegetables. Put a container of vitamin and mineral tablets where you cannot forget them - perhaps next to your toothbrush, so you remember to take one every day. And make it a point to buy more fruits and vegetable at the grocery store. You will only ever eat what you buy, so if you control your purchases, you will necessarily control your eating and drinking habits. Taking these small steps will go a long way towards creating a physical body capable of focus on passion, purpose and vision. Make a list of the steps you will take to make these changes, and after at least two weeks of implementing the changes in your life, record the differences you feel within yourself.

*"there is no greater advice for you than that which lies within your own heart."*

Application Idea:  The first step to following your heart is learning how to listen to it.  Try quieting your mind even if it is for only ten or fifteen minutes.  Let your thoughts pass through your mind, without dwelling on or attaching to them.  During this quiet period, ask yourself a question that most troubles you, and ask it without an answer in mind.  Try to clear your head and let the response come to you unprovoked by your brain.  A good technique to facilitate this process is to ask the question in writing with your right hand (if you are right handed), but answer the question with your left hand without thinking about the answer or worrying about your handwriting.  Just put down what immediately comes to mind.  The left hand is controlled by the right brain, which is the more creative, intuitive center in the brain.  The responses that are generated here, although they may not make great logical sense, represent where your heart is on the matter.  Write down the interaction, the questions and the responses.

*"the voice within is the loudest voice with which the heart speaks, but often is the hardest for us to hear. this voice comes from your essence. listen carefully to it, and obey it and you will create profound happiness and authentic power."*

Application Idea: The voice within is our intuition. It is a sense of knowing the direction we need to take, or the choice we need to make, without necessarily knowing the reason why. Following our intuition leads us to grace and a flow of life that seems almost effortless. Denying or ignoring our intuition often leads us difficulty, pain, anxiety and a path that is usually marked by struggle. Intuition, on the other hand, comes in peace, or joy, or love. It does not come with negative emotions. Negative emotions are the domain of fear. If you want to know the answer to a question about your life and the direction you should take, ask yourself the question in a moment when you are alone and can be quiet. Then try and identify the answer by your feelings and the body reactions that accompany each potential response. Do you feel tight in your chest, or do you feel a lump in your throat, as you consider different answers? Or do you experience feelings of peace, lightness or freedom? If so, then you can be sure your intuition is guiding you. Your job is to trust that intuition and follow it, even though you may not have "objective" evidence to support the choice. Record the questions you have and the physical sensations in your body that arise as you consider different responses to those questions.

*"who do you choose to be now?"*

# AUTHENTIC

*"personal honesty is, in reality, an issue of self-love. if you have difficulty being completely honest with yourself and others, then you cannot love yourself completely. it signifies that there is a part of you that you do not love, or that you despise, and your shame about that part causes you to hide it from others with dishonesty. to become truly happy and at peace with yourself, you must learn to become completely honest."*

Application Idea: Being honest about who you are is simply saying to yourself and others that "what I think and feel is good, it is me." A good test to determine whether or not you are comfortable with who you are, is to ask yourself this simple question. Do you allow anyone and everyone to know anything or everything about you? And I really mean everything, including your past. If you answer no, it is clear you have work to do. Begin to examine the areas of your life where you do not present the truth to others. Identify the fears you have around disclosing the truth, and ask yourself how real those fears are. Then identify an area or a subject about which you have been untruthful, and make it a point to venture into the realm of being truthful about it. Bring it up in a discussion with someone this week that it is difficult to tell the truth to, and take a risk. If you are really courageous, see if you can go one whole week telling the complete truth to everyone that you speak to. If you catch yourself lying or failing to disclose the truth, correct yourself publicly and tell the other party what the real truth is. Record your experiences being truthful. Telling the complete truth may be extremely difficult for you to do, but the rewards are great. You will find that telling the truth creates freedom, and freedom is the key to permanent happiness.

*"intention never matures into purpose or accomplishment, without realization through action."*

Application Idea: The clearest indicator of our "truth" is what we do, not what we say. So many people say one thing, but then do another, or never do what they talk about. Without action, our intentions never see the light of day. To realize your purpose in life you must begin to put your intentions into action. It does not need to be a grand plan that occupies all of your time. Even spending fifteen to thirty minutes a day to pursue your dream will make a huge difference. Over time, that small investment will lead to the accomplishment of big goals. Begin to put into action something that you have been talking about doing, but as of yet have not done. Perhaps it is writing a book, creating a song or a painting, building something, or starting a new business. Whatever it is, identify it, write down the goal, and then make a point to spend at least fifteen minutes every day doing something in furtherance of it. If you miss a day, or change your goal, don't get down on yourself, just treat each day as a new one and start again.

*"relationships are the vehicles by which we learn who we are and decide who we want to be."*

Application Idea: Although it is difficult for many people to accept, people show up in our lives to teach us who we are. If you want to know what it is you need to learn and accept about yourself, take a look around you and identify the type of people in your life. If you see a lot of anger, it is because you are angry and have not yet learned to accept that part of yourself. If you live in a world of fear, it is because you are fearful. If you see a lot of sadness, it is because you are sad. Whatever themes you see in your life, you can be sure that life is presenting these people and you are attracting them into your life so that you will learn about that trait in yourself and be presented with a choice of how you will respond. That choice, the choice of response, is where you have the opportunity to decide who it is you are and want to be. Make a list of the personality or character traits of people who consistently show up in your life that you do not like. Try to be as general as possible, referring to the qualities or traits rather than the specific behaviors that represent them. Once you have made this list, then identify the ways in which you are like them. This may take some deep thinking on your part, for often the evidence is not obvious. The more clever we are, the more clever our egos have to be to disguise the traits and hide them from our view. But they are there if you will look closely. If you have a hard time seeing these traits in yourself, then ask those who are close to you to tell you honestly whether or not you ever demonstrate these traits, and if so how. They will help you see what you cannot. Awareness is the first step we must take in becoming who we want to be, and this exercise will help you identify the parts of yourself that prefer to remain hidden from view.

*"our willingness to be completely honest with ourselves and others creates an upward spiral of confidence and security that magnifies immeasurably our self worth."*

Application Idea: Lack of trust and honesty is the primary destroyer of self-esteem and of all relationships. When we fail ourselves by being deceitful and dishonest, we declare to the world that who we are is not good enough. Otherwise there would be no need to lie. If we truly love and value ourselves, despite out weaknesses and issues, then we are free to present exactly who we are to the world without compromise or misrepresentation. Make a list of people with whom you are not being completely honest and what it is that you are lying to them about. Make sure your list is complete and includes those people to whom, although you might not be directly lying, you are not disclosing the whole or complete truth. Be honest in this exercise and dare to be complete. Then, make it a goal to speak to everyone in your life who is operating with false assumptions about you and who you are, so you can tell them the complete truth. This task is difficult, and you will undoubtedly come up with all kinds of justifications and excuses why you do not need to be, or should not be, honest. The biggest one of all, of course, is that you don't want to hurt someone, or you are protecting someone from something they don't really need to know anyway. These are manipulations of the ego that prevent you from facing yourself. If I asked you whether or not you would ever want someone in relationship with you to lie to you or not disclose some material fact that may affect your relationship, to protect you, I am quite sure you would tell me no. You would want to face the truth no matter how painful so that you could make a conscious and powerful choice about the relationship. This fact is true for everyone else as well. Lying to someone about who we are, or not disclosing the truth, is a manipulation that strips others of the power to make conscious choices about their relationships with us. So let go of the illusion that you are ever protecting anyone by denying them the truth. Stepping up means having the courage to be real. Despite the initial pain you might feel, you will be surprised how being honest will build your self-esteem, contribute to your sense of freedom and self-love, and how it can positively and dramatically change your life.

*"who do you choose to be now?"*

# IMAGINATIVE

*"beginning today, you should begin to think of yourself as that which you wish to become. thoughts always precede action and without imagining positive changes in yourself, such changes become more difficult to realize."*

Application idea: Science has proven in the laboratory that thoughts create a change in energy, not only in our own cells, but also in the particles and energy that surround us. Thus, positive changes in form, whether internal or external, must begin with changes to your own mental perceptions. Write down something about yourself (either physical, mental or spiritual) that you normally view negatively or comment negatively about, and make it an objective to see it in a new way. Spend some time with the trait or characteristic and try to find ways that it serves your life. Then, begin to change your language and actions around that trait or characteristic. Make it a point to discuss the trait or characteristic publicly, stating something positive about it and what it has contributed to your life. Cease making negative remarks about it, and focus your thoughts, words and actions on being someone who is not burdened by the trait or negative perception. Engage in those activities and have the thoughts that such a person as that which you are trying to become would have. We become who we dream of being, when we are willing to be it. So start by being it now.

*"an active body facilitates an active mind and spirit."*

Application Idea:  The many, many benefits of exercise are well proven and thus do not require much discussion.  More important, I believe, is the discussion of how we can implement exercise in our lives, and what we should do.  I try to follow a very simple rule for exercise.  Trust your body enough to indicate to you what kinds of exercise you should engage in, and do what you are attracted to doing.  We do not need to enslave ourselves into a torturous training program that leaves us in pain and unmotivated to do more.  Rather, we can find activities that we enjoy, and mix our activities up every day rather than get stuck in some boring routine.  Write down a list of all of the physical activities that you enjoy.  Exhaust your list, including anything that gets your heart rate up.  Make it a point each day to do something from your list, even if it is only for twenty minutes or so.  Any amount of exercise above what you are doing today will improve your state of well-being.  If you miss a day, don't fret.  We are not proving anything here, and it is not an ego-centered goal we are after.  We are simply trying to create an active body that can support the energy necessary to be creative, visionary and intuitive.

*"life is one grand dichotomy and those that see the negative in it and those that see the positive in it are both right, for life presents both sides. the question you must decide for yourself, therefore, is which will you choose to perceive, acknowledge, and give your power to."*

Application Idea: Many people care more about being right in life, than being happy, in love, having peace, etc. So they spend all of their time and energy trying to prove the "correctness" of their position, rather than using that time and energy to be constructive, creative and find solutions to the issues that block their progress. You must decide right now how important being right to you really is. There are many lonely, depressed, angry and unproductive individuals in this world who are right. They care more about proving their perceptions and positions, than they do in building relationships that will benefit their life. Make a list of the people, places and things in your life that have been triggering negative feelings within you. Then make a simple decision. Do you wish to continue to have that person, place or thing continue as a part of your life? If the answer is no, make an effort this week to terminate your relationship with that person, place or thing. Let it go, and don't look back. If, however, the answer is yes, then try to identify what is positive about the relationship and how you can maximize it in your life. Make it a point to verbalize to any individuals in these relationships the value you do see in them, and your effort to try and improve the relationship. Elicit their support in this effort. Then, keep your focus on what the person, place or circumstance can contribute to your life and how you can give back in a constructive way.

*"do not allow yourself to be limited by "conventional wisdom" or traditional notions, for they do not represent the outer limits of what is possible, rather they are merely the outer limits of past dreams."*

Application Idea: So many people allow their thinking to be confined by popular opinions or what other people believe, and thus miss out on the realization of their dreams or big ideas. In reality, this is an issue of validation and acceptance and those that allow themselves to be confined in this way value acceptance more than they value originality, creativity or imagination. Everyone who has ever imagined something and tried to create it, first had to be willing to risk their idea being misunderstood and/or rejected. Identify and record an area of your life that you believe needs some imaginative thinking. Perhaps it is a business idea, or something you want to create like a book, a song or a painting, or perhaps it is a relationship you want to improve. Identify what that area of your life would look like in an ideal situation. Try to see it in your mind as ideal or perfect and then write down what that looks like for you. Then find ten people you can ask this question to: if you were to set out to achieve this objective (identify your ideal situation that you want to create), what would you do? Try to identify ten people that are totally different than you. Remember, you should not be looking for validation here, but rather new, imaginative ideas. So try to find people who you think are creative and who look at life differently than you do. And listen to their answers. Don't judge or criticize them, but see if they have merit or if they can at least inspire you to think of something new that you have not thought of before.

*"who do you choose to be now?"*

# COMPASSIONATE

*"judgment weakens us and robs us of authentic power when we use it to reaffirm a perception or view that we are bad, or not worthy of success in life. the fact is that past actions and choices that do not represent who we now want to be were, and are, necessary for our growth and development. they do not define who we are and always will be, but rather are teachers of who and what we are now not. For that reason they are to be embraced and appreciated for the growth experiences they are."*

Application Idea:  I want you to begin to examine closely the things about you that you judge most harshly.  Perhaps it is something you did when you were younger, a behavior that you are ashamed of or feel guilty about.  Perhaps it is an aspect of your personality today that you are not proud of, that you try to keep hidden from others because you think it is bad or wrong.  Maybe it is anger or depression or anxiety, or the feeling that you are weak or too emotional.  Whatever it is, I want you to take a fresh new look at it.  Start by identifying the trait or behavior that you judge as being bad.  But this time, as you review it in your mind, let go of your judgments about it.  No matter how bad you might think it is, I want you to try and identify at least five great things about the behavior that have brought happiness to your life, and have caused you to grow.  This exercise will require you to go deep, and to spend some time examining how these "wrong choices," as you may view them, have really served you and helped you become who you are today or who it is you want to be.  This exercise will help you become compassionate with yourself.  And the more compassionate you are with yourself, the more compassionate you will be with others.

*"do not get down on yourself for acting in ways you believe are wrong. even when it seems clear that you have acted in a way that is less than your potential, have faith that on another day, perhaps tomorrow, you will choose to represent yourself as the highest expression of what and who you really are."*

Application Idea:  Life is a process and a journey, not a destination or an achievement.  We have all heard that expression before, but it is worthy of remembering.  It is okay to act in fear.  It is okay to be weak, to be insecure, to feel jealousy, anger, depression, upset or anxiety.  It does not mean that you are a weak or insecure or depressed person because you have these feelings.  These kinds of emotions are an integral part of human life.  We all have them.  If we reject or deny them, they come back even stronger, demanding our attention.  If we accept and embrace them, then they are content to pass through us, having no need to make a home. I want you to develop and outline in writing a symbolic ritual of acceptance that you can employ whenever you are feeling down or weak or depressed or less than whole.  Have this ritual first acknowledge and honor the negative feelings or emotions that you are experiencing.  Second, include within the ritual a time for identifying in writing the value to your life that these negative feelings or emotions bring.  You may have to really think about this one.  Finally, conclude the ritual with a symbolic gesture that allows you to release the feelings or emotions and let them go.  Honoring all of your emotions and feelings in this way will allow you to find perfection in the imperfection and allow your compassion to grow infinitely.

*"one of our objectives must be, not the destruction of variation in the conditions of life, but rather to recognize unity in spite of these variations. to recognize that spark of greatness that exists in each of us regardless of our condition, and despite differences that we may not understand or that we may fear."*

Application Idea: It is easy to notice great things in great people. It is easy to see that which we like in people, places or things that are pleasing. It is much more difficult to notice and observe that special something about someone who is different than we are, or who manifests less desirable qualities. Nevertheless, all people do have strengths and great qualities. Your lack of ability to see them is a reflection of your deficiency, not theirs. Your task is to identify someone (perhaps you know them, perhaps you don't) that you find less than desirable. Try to find something about them that you like, something that you can genuinely admire. This might take some time on your part really getting to know them. But try to find the common ground between you and them that could be the basis for a constructive relationship. Then make an effort to actually converse with the person and relate to them on the common ground or admirable qualities that you have identified. Tell them what you admire about them and let them know the value that you see in them. Doing so will help change their world, and yours. Record the experience you have fulfilling this exercise.

*"the greatest aspect of our individuality is that we all have the ability to positively affect different people.  where I may have no effect on a certain person, you may change their life forever.  likewise, where your experiences and gifts may not touch the soul of an individual, perhaps mine will.  this is the power of our uniqueness and individuality."*

Application Idea:  It is rumored that Butch Harmon, Tiger Wood's golf coach, was once asked what Tiger Woods' greatest weakness was as a golfer and what he did about it.  Butch replied that his greatest weakness was hitting out of sand traps.  When asked what he did about it, Butch had an interesting reply.  He said while most coaches would work with a golfer to try and enhance their ability to get out of the trap, Butch noted that Tiger was one of the best in golf at hitting the fairway and not going into the sand trap in the first place.  So, he said, his strategy was to work with Tiger's strengths of hitting fairways and staying out of sand traps in the first place, rather than working with his weakness.  The result?  Tiger became the best player in the world.  Sometimes we spend too much time trying to overcome our weaknesses, instead of leveraging our strengths.  Write down a list of your specific and unique skills and abilities.  Evaluate whether you are leveraging these strengths in your work, life, and your relationships.  Try to identify several activities you are not currently doing that would better utilize your strengths and bring greater value and benefit to your life and the lives of others.

*"the truly loving being is not the one who intends to be loving, or talks or thinks about love, but rather is the one who acts lovingly and compassionately."*

Application Idea: Being loving and compassionate is not a passive experience, it is an active one. It requires our intention and our effort. Most people have loving thoughts and intentions, but fewer translate those thoughts and intentions into loving action. Yet our choices and our actions are the clearest and most reliable indicator of our truth. Without loving and compassionate actions, therefore, it is likely that we are not as loving and as compassionate as we might like to believe. Identify and record one way in which you could consistently extend yourself solely for the benefit of someone else. Perhaps it is volunteering at a hospital, a charity or a community organization. Or it could be in making a concerted effort to help someone you know achieve a goal that they believe is important. Whatever it is, choose an action that requires ongoing activity on your part, and will create a tangible benefit to the recipient and make this activity a part of your life. In so doing, you will translate loving thoughts and intentions into tangible loving actions and feelings, both in others and yourself.

# *"love's first requirement is that it be given to ourselves."*

Application Idea: You cannot give away that which you don't have. If I am to teach you about physics, I must first learn about physics. If I am to give you money, I must first acquire the money to give you. The same is true for love. To be loving human beings, we must first acquire it for ourselves. The biggest hurdle most people have in loving themselves is that they often think it is selfish to spend time or money or attention on themselves. They have to be doing something for others to feel good about who they are. This too is an act of selfishness, just a different one that often leads to anger and resentment because too often it demands the acceptance and appreciation of others for the gift given. Real love demands nothing of others. It gives for love's sake, and nothing more. But for love to be given freely, you must have lots of it, and only you can give yourself the love that you need. So, today, make it a point to do something for yourself that you really enjoy. Perhaps it is getting a massage or facial, working on a favorite project or hobby, or going for a walk or long run. Whatever it is, make time for you and don't let others make you feel guilty for doing so. Write down a list of activities that you really enjoy doing and that nurture and sustain you. Then, make sure that your daily schedule affords you some time for yourself, doing at least one of the things that you love to do each day. In loving yourself first, you will create the basis upon which you can love others more freely.

*"I love because I choose to and want to, not because I need to. I love for the joy that loving brings me and others, not for the return of love. If others love me in return, then I am blessed and I appreciate such love. If others do not return my love, it does not matter, for by the very act of loving I have defined who it is I am and want to be."*

Application Idea: The expression of unconditional love towards another human being is the most elevated action a human being can take. In simple terms, when we manifest unconditional love towards others we are acting in greatness. And when we act in greatness, we will feel great. It takes hard work to get to a place where we can love others unconditionally and act compassionately towards them. It requires first that you love and are compassionate with yourself, because you can't give away anything that you don't have. Once you have done this, however, then you can begin to express that love and compassion towards others. Be observant of your circumstances and interactions with others and try to identify a person or a circumstance where you can "love first." Perhaps it is with a stranger who acts fearfully towards you. Perhaps it is a work or personal situation where you have the opportunity to act in a loving way for no reason, or for no expectation of return. Whatever the situation, make a decision to "love first" and notice how you can change your world by being the change you want to see. Write down your experience with this practice.

*"who do you choose to be now?"*

# COURAGEOUS

*"to become truly happy and at peace, you must learn to stand back and be yourself. you must learn to free yourself from the outside influences that overshadow you and learn to rid yourself of attachment to outside approval. the only approval that matters, that can generate true happiness, is the approval of self. approval of self is manifested, not by saying or thinking that you like yourself, but by taking the risk to be yourself, even in the face of opposition from family, friends and peers."*

Application Idea: Try to make a conscious choice today to say or do one thing publicly that is truly you, but that might shock people in your life who have known you for years and who would expect different behavior from you. Make it a point to push yourself, and ignore the fears in your head that may tell you how foolish, or wrong you are to be yourself. Of course, your choice should not be something that would be illegal, or would physically hurt another person. Rather it should simply be a choice that reflects who you really are, a part of yourself that you have kept hidden from others because of fears that you would not be accepted for manifesting it. Some examples might be singing out loud in public, if you like to sing, or telling a person your true feelings without regard to their reactions. Or perhaps you might ask someone for something you really want or need from them, even if it feels difficult to do so. The point here is to stretch yourself in to being yourself. Then notice afterwards the feelings of peace and freedom and joy it generates. Write down your experience.

*"where you find joy and laughter, so too will you find a body and a mind that can heal itself."*

Application Idea: We have forgotten how to laugh and be silly. We take ourselves far too seriously and put too much stock into what others think about us. Time to end that. Time to learn the value of silly. Spend some time in observation of children between the ages of three and five years old. It can be your own kids, or the children of a family member or the children of a friend, but try to spend at least fifteen or twenty minutes of quality observation time, really watching how they have fun. Record your observations. Children are spontaneous, they laugh easily, and they have fun because they don't yet care what other people think. If they are hurt, then they cry but quickly return to laughter and play. What a beautiful approach to life. After you have observed their behavior, then your task is to follow their example and be goofy and silly yourself. Try to do at least one thing that others would judge or do judge as being silly or immature. Sing out loud, make faces, dance outrageously, do something that is out of character for you, and notice how it makes you feel alive afterward. Make a note of your experience and the feelings that it generates.

*"response-ability is the vision to see how we create all of the circumstances of our lives, and the courage to step up and change the ones that do not define who it is we want to be."*

Application Idea: Responsibility is exactly what the parts of the word mean when defined individually: it is the "ability to respond." Responsibility does not mean beating ourselves up, judging ourselves, or admitting failure. It simply means that we have the power and ability to respond to any situation or person in a new or different way, to create a new or different result. Take a good hard look at your life. Write down the areas of your life where you are not happy, where you are not fulfilled, and where you are not being who it is that you believe you want to be. Identify the steps you would need to take to change those circumstances and be the person you want to be. Then make the decision today to take responsibility for your life and create the outcomes and results that you keep waiting for others to produce for you. Wait no longer for others to deliver the results or dreams you have for yourself, but rather become your own advocate, supporter and motivator. Act now. The fulfillment of your dreams and your passion is waiting.

*"when we can smile and create joy, we begin to deflate our problems. when we deflate our problems, we heal them. when we heal our problems, we heal ourselves. when we heal ourselves, we heal the world."*

Application Idea:  Smiling has the ability to greatly affect the moods and attitudes of everyone around you. Smiles are infectious, and it is difficult for people not to smile back at you when you smile at them.  Make it a point to smile whenever and wherever you can.  At whomever you can.  In particular, make it a point the next time someone around you is being unhappy, to look at them, grab them by the face if you know them and it is appropriate, smile at them, and tell them something you like about them.  Doing so, you will create a vastly different experience than if you simply respond by reflecting their unhappy moods.  Write down your experience, noting the feelings this action generates in you and in the other person.

*"love is everything. love forms the basis for every gen-uine moment of our lives: our birth, our death, our sensu-ality, our passion, our truth, our suffering, our happiness, our living and our dying. all of these are constructed out of love. everything else is just an illusion and a distraction from love."*

Application Idea: Whatever circumstance we find ourselves in, no matter who we are dealing with, we ele-vate ourselves and others when we seek to be loving. True leadership is the province of people who have the ability to rise above the pettiness or fear of a circumstance or a person, and respond with love. History hon-ors, reveres and remembers most, he or she who has learned the power of love and the ability to see beyond the fears and illusions of people or circumstances. Whether at work, at play, or wherever you may be, try to be the catalyst for the transformation of people or circumstances around you. Perhaps it will be with someone speak-ing angrily or fearfully with you or others, or it will be a work or family situation where the participants are acting out of fear and ignorance and clearly forgetting the importance and value of the relationship and the big-ger picture. Whatever the situation, take it upon yourself to infuse a loving and peaceful attitude in response to the situation, and see if you can change the outcome with your loving participation in it. Experiment with your responses and record the experiences you have and the reactions you receive. The more you try, the bet-ter you will become, so don't get frustrated if your attempts seem unsuccessful. Often the results generated from loving action are unseen, and come later, after the participants have had a chance to peacefully reflect on your loving contributions.

*"no one but you can play your music and you cannot genuinely play the music of another. you must find your own music, your own path, and your own adventure. to do this, you must of course find yourself first. then, the only question becomes whether or not you will say yes to your adventure and to playing your music."*

Application Idea: It takes a lot of courage to be yourself and pursue your dreams. It is not an easy path to take. We often have to walk against the flow of life and popular opinion to authentically be ourselves. But history is replete with examples of individuals who changed the world by their willingness to spend much of their life outside of the approval of the world, pursuing their own ideas and dreams. To be sure, following our destiny is certainly not the path of comfort and security. But if you can muster the courage to say yes to your adventure and follow your dreams, then you pave the way for others to do the same. This is true leadership, vision and passion. And everyone is capable of achieving it. It simply requires that you make the choice to do so. Write down who you would be, and what you would do with your life if you had everything that you wanted or needed: the perfect relationships, all of the money and security you needed, and the opportunity to do it. Then, pretend that you do. Pretend that you have everything that you need to do this thing and be this person. Identify in writing what such a person would do with their life, what choices they would make day to day, and what activities they would accomplish. Then go for it. Live as if you have already arrived at where you want to be. Be the person that you dream of, and do the things that you have only dreamed about doing. Make your dream a reality today.

*"The gifts of authentic power that we are developing in you through this program, gifts like passion, vision, and purpose, will come when you learn to live where they are found in abundance:  right here, right now, in the present moment.  Not in some illusionary place seeking something that is not true for you right now, or in a previous present moment that no longer is, but rather right here in this moment where life is unfolding before you.  It is here that the resolution we seek is ultimately found."*

# WHO HAVE YOU BECOME?

*"let the world know what you stand for, and who you have become."*

As we mature or go through life-changing periods of time, it is often difficult to detect changes within ourselves. Because we live in the myopia of our bodies and our minds day in and day out, it is harder to see the aggregate consequence of our internal change. However, one way in which we do get to "see" our changes is through the eyes of those around us. We experience ourselves through our relationship to others.

After spending several weeks in my program, clients who I work with personally begin to show up to their appointments in different ways than when they begin. Typically, I start to see their "inner spirit" emerging. I notice that they are happier, more peaceful, and much more positive and optimistic about their futures. While they still have issues and challenges that they need to work through, their issues have less dramatic impact on their lives, and they begin to feel more capable of achieving great things despite them. It is not uncommon for my clients to begin reporting greater feelings of freedom and a deeper calmness in their life; happiness, focus and clarity; and more profound love and compassion towards others.

Following a few more weeks of the work, things typically become exciting. People start to get glimpses of who they really are, and what they are truly capable of achieving. They begin to sense their real, authentic power. And when they do the heavens open up and creative ideas, passionate goals and aspirations, and visionary perspectives come raining down.

By now, if you have taken the time to work through all of the exercises of this program, you are probably starting to feel some of these same changes in yourself. More remarkably, you are probably starting to have people around you, and close to you, noticing changes in you and commenting about them. You have done a lot of difficult internal work, and now you are beginning to experience some of the rewards associated with that work. For this reason, it is time to celebrate and notice who you are today.

The purpose of this final section is to help you stand back and see who you have become. It includes a few of the same questions you answered in the beginning of the program, because I want you to see how you have changed and how your responses today are different, and how they represent the new person that you are.

It also asks you to define your "Principles of Being." I have included my "Principles of Being" so you can get an idea of what I mean by this request. But I don't want you to copy mine. Rather I want you to set forth your own principles, and the ideas that mean the most to you. These should be the principles and ideas that you believe in, that you are passionate about, and for which you want your life to be defined.

These principles are not meant to be stagnant. They will change over time, and that is okay. You change also. Nor are these principles meant to be a statement that "you are these things, all of the time." I certainly know that I do not embody all of the time everything that I aspire to be. Yet it is important to have a map of who it is I want to be, and writing these principles down has helped me keep that in mind, so I can practice "being" it today. So go ahead and write out the ideas and principles that mean the most to you. Then make cards of them, and share them with anyone and everyone you can.

*life balance reassessment*

On a scale of 1 to 10, with 1 being Dismal and 10 being Fantastic, rate the following areas of your life:

**Family Life**

| 1 | 2 | 3 | 4 | 5 | 6 | 7 | 8 | 9 | 10 |

**Business Life**

| 1 | 2 | 3 | 4 | 5 | 6 | 7 | 8 | 9 | 10 |

**Social Life**

| 1 | 2 | 3 | 4 | 5 | 6 | 7 | 8 | 9 | 10 |

**Spiritual Life**

| 1 | 2 | 3 | 4 | 5 | 6 | 7 | 8 | 9 | 10 |

**Financial Life**

| 1 | 2 | 3 | 4 | 5 | 6 | 7 | 8 | 9 | 10 |

**Fun Life**

| 1 | 2 | 3 | 4 | 5 | 6 | 7 | 8 | 9 | 10 |

**Personal Mission In Life**

| 1 | 2 | 3 | 4 | 5 | 6 | 7 | 8 | 9 | 10 |

**Energy Life**

| 1 | 2 | 3 | 4 | 5 | 6 | 7 | 8 | 9 | 10 |

**Physical Health**

| 1 | 2 | 3 | 4 | 5 | 6 | 7 | 8 | 9 | 10 |

How happy are you on a scale of 1 - 10: ____. If less than 10, what would you need in your life to be a ten?

_____

_____

_____

_____

_____

List the three characteristics of life that you desire most (e.g., peace, love, security, wisdom, excitement, etc.)

_____

_____

_____

_____

_____

Would your friends, family, and peers describe you any differently today than before you started this program?

_____

_____

_____

_____

_____

How do you define success today?

_____

_____

_____

_____

_____

Have your business, health, family, primary relationship and emotional well-being goals for this year changed at all?   If so how, and what are they now?

_____

_____

_____

_____

_____

_____

What are your thoughts consistently focused on today?

_____

_____

_____

_____

_____

Who have you become?

_____

_____

_____

_____

_____

_____

_____

_____

_____

_____

_____

_____

_____

## *principles of being*

I acknowledge that every circumstance and relationship in my life is a direct or indirect result of choices I have made, or failed to make. I understand that I am the supreme creator of my life and everything in it, and I choose every day to accept my present circumstances and relationships exactly as they are, unless I am consciously acting to change them.

I believe that life is exactly as we choose to see it. All people, places and things can present both a negative and positive perspective. We, as observers, make the choice of what we see. Because I want to fill my life with joy, I choose to recognize beauty in all things.

I will try to have every choice I make be consistent with the highest vision I have of myself. Rather than try to control or manipulate others to conform to my addictive behaviors or programming, I will allow others to simply be, and will learn to change my addictions into preferences. I know this is the only way I can be truly happy.

I know it is better to live my life without expectations or attachment to results. Although I may plan for the future, I must not become too attached to the fulfillment of those plans or I may miss other more fulfilling opportunities. If life takes me in a direction different than the one I have planned, I believe it is for my ultimate good.

I want to approach each and every moment of every day with enthusiasm, happiness, passion and present-moment focus. Life and everything in it, is a wonderful experience that I know I must appreciate, using all of my senses to fully enjoy it.

Honesty is one of the single greatest principles in life, and I will approach every person, circumstance or situation with a commitment to be honest with myself, to openly and honestly present my true thoughts and feelings to others, and to never lie, deceive or mislead another person.

I believe in being sensitive, and before acting or reacting to any situation or person, I will try my best to act or react in a way that I would want to be treated under the same circumstances.

I cannot judge any person, situation or thing for I do not know all of the facts. My experience with anything is limited to my interaction with that person, situation or thing - and that is not the complete picture. Therefore, I cannot judge whether anything or anyone is good or bad, right or wrong. I also know I should not judge myself harshly, for I am a learning, loving human being that can draw strength from all of my experiences.

I recognize that I can only view life through my own rose-colored glasses, and the beliefs, opinions or standards of any group or person, including my own, are not necessarily universal truths.

I have a thirst and love for knowledge and understanding, and I recognize that true learning and growth comes only from effort, experience and a willingness to accept some new ideas, even if it means the rejection of previously-held beliefs.

I love living and I know that a healthy body is an essential part of maintaining the quality of my life experience. Consequently, I will exercise my body and will feed it with healthy air, food and drink. I will heal it and rest it when necessary, and I will treat my body with loving care. I will touch others and smile often, for it is my true nature to be kind. I will also laugh a lot.

I believe in God, Spirit, or the Soul - whatever name we give to that power in the universe that exists beyond our obvious senses. Life becomes magical when we see the clues that spirit offers and I will strive to find them. I also know that inviting Spirit into my life allows me to make better choices than I would otherwise make, for it allows me to view life from the perspective of heaven.

I believe that each of us can contribute to the world in some unique way. For me, it is to share with others the principles that I hold dear, in the hope that these principles will benefit others as much as they have given benefit to me. I am fulfilled and happy when I act in service to others.

The real purpose of life is love. Love is our very essence, the all which created us and is us. This day I will work to remove that which blocks my love from flowing freely. I will learn to love myself and I will liberally share my love with others. I will be kind, understanding and compassionate. I will make love a daily focus and priority in my life, and I will try to fill every moment of my life and yours with love.

STEPTHREE

## *your principles of being*

I believe that

_____

_____

_____

_____

_____

_____

I believe that

_____

_____

_____

_____

_____

_____

I know that

_____

_____

_____

_____

_____

_____

I know that

_____

_____

_____

_____

_____

I understand

_____

_____

_____

_____

_____

I understand

_____

_____

_____

_____

_____

I will

_____

_____

_____

_____

_____

## *a final note and challenge*

If you think about it, life boils down simply in three ways: relationship to the moment, relationship to the self, and relationship to others. All experiences in life fall into one of these three categories, and usually into all three of them at the same time.

In this program I have tried to help you develop all three forms. Many of the exercises had you take inventory of what each of your senses was experiencing in the present moment, and had you identify the parts of "now" that bring beauty to your life. This focus on the present moment teaches us to value and appreciate the only thing in life that is real - the moment that is happening right now.

We also closely examined who we really are through provocative questions, and we discussed principles like truth, courage, vision and passion, and practiced exercises to develop these traits. These principles, questions and exercises help us learn who we are in relationship to ourselves, and help us develop qualities that ultimately create authenticity, compassion and personal well-being. They do so because they help us relate successfully to ourselves and to the moment, and they fill us with a sense of greatness that comes from living to principles bigger than we are.

Finally, we investigated our relationships with others and looked at ways of perceiving value in them, even if they are difficult. We discussed how relationships are the mirrors by which we define who we are, and who we choose to be. Whether it be with friends, partners, enemies, co-workers, bosses, or unknown people behind store windows and in taxis, we are the sum experience of our relationships and all of them serve to reflect back a world that exists within us.

Sir Edmund Hillary, the first man to ever climb Mount Everest, once stated: "it is not the mountain that we conquer, but ourselves." He understood that the ability to ascend the highest mountain in the world had less to do with the mountain, and more to do with the character of the man or woman attempting to ascend it. What is true about mountains is also true for us. All external things, whether they are mountains or people in our lives, exist to provide us with an opportunity to learn about who we are, and to ascend through our fears and limitations. Thus, in our lives, "it is not the relationships or circumstances that we conquer, but ourselves."

We spend so much of our time thinking about the people who are in our lives, and wondering why they act the way they do. All of this thought distracts us from the real issue at hand, which is us. It is never really about who is in your life and what they do. Rather, the real issue that should occupy your mind is who are you in relationship to the people in your life?

Relationships are the means by which we get to see who we are. What we see in them, generally and specifically, is what exists within us. It takes much wisdom and experience to understand this. Our egos and minds are very clever, and they create complex stories and illusions that help us to believe that other people are different than we are. This belief feeds our dramas and our stories that we are either better than others, or not as good. The truth is we are neither, we are all equal manifestations of that divine power and intelligence that is responsible for our creation, and the entire world of human experiences, all of it - the good, the bad, the ugly and the beautiful, exists within each of us.

Relationships are also the means by which we get to choose who we will be. In response to any action, word or thought of another, will we choose to respond in love or fear? Our ability to respond to others with truth, compassion, and courage, especially when they are acting in fear, is the meter by which our readiness to be great can be measured. If we respond in kind to people acting in fear, or to fearful circumstances, then it is clear we have work still to do. When we are able to see the fear of others, however, and respond with kindness, truth and compassion, then we are able to contribute something of significance and value to them. This is the foundation of successful relationship. When we can do this habitually, we are beginning to live a life that can have a serious positive impact on the lives of others.

Through this program you have been developing principles like passion, vision and authentic power, and hopefully you have had the opportunity to see dramatic changes occur in your life. Stepping up required you to "see" the opportunity to change your life and act upon it. And you did so, and in so doing have set into motion a chain of events and consequences that will contribute to your life for years to come.

However, stepping up to our greatness and to a position of leadership in this world also requires that we share our gifts and provide others with opportunities to develop passion, vision and authentic power in their lives. That is your final challenge in this program. To take the opportunity you have had and share it with others. To be an example to others of what they can become if they learn and do what you have learned to do.

Identify three people you think could change their lives by following this program. Write down their names and addresses on the sheet provided below. Write them a note in the space provided telling them how you feel about them, how your life has changed, and why you want them to experience the changes you have had as a result of this program. Sign the note in the space provided and then send the list and notes into us, along with payment for the programs.

We will send each of them a program along with your note, and we will donate a fourth program to the charitable organization of your choice, so that someone else receives a program that would otherwise not be able to afford it.

Stepping up to this final challenge will help you help us change the lives of the people you care about the most, and the people who need it most.

**I WANT YOU TO HELP ME CHANGE THE LIVES OF THE FOLLOWING PEOPLE:**

1. Name and Address:_____

_____

_____

Personal Note to them: _____

_____

_____

2. Name and Address:_____

_____

_____

Personal Note to them: _____

_____

_____

3. Name and Address:_____

_____

_____

Personal Note to them: _____

_____

_____

4. Name and address of charitable organization to receive program donated in your

name:_____

_____

_____

**PLEASE MAIL TO:**    **QUANTUM HORIZONS, LLC.**

**1730 E. WARNER RD., SUITE 10-142**

**TEMPE, ARIZONA 85284**

**PHONE: 1.800.930.8837**

# QuantumHorizons

## *"guiding the development and vision of people and organizations"*

Quantum Horizons, LLC

1730 E. Warner Road

Suite 10-142

Tempe, Arizona 85284

Fax: 480.491.7225

Email: austinvickers@cox.net

www.austinvickers.com

**PRODUCT ORDER FORM**

By Fax with a credit card: fill in the following order form and fax to: 480-491-7225

By Mail with a check: please make payable to Quantum Horizons, LLC and send to address above.

For volume discounts, please contact us at: 1-800-930-8837

Paid by: Visa _____ Mastercard _____ American Express _____ Check _____

Card Number: _____ Expiration Date: _____/_____/_____

Name of Cardholder: _____

Phone: (_____) _____ Fax: (_____) _____

Signature of Cardholder: _____ Date: _____/_____/_____

Ship to Address: _____

City: _____ State/Prov.: _____ Zip Code: _____

Country: _____ Email address: _____

| QUANTITY | ITEM | DESCRIPTION | TAXABLE | WHLS. PRICE | TOTAL |
|----------|------|-------------|---------|-------------|-------|
| | | The "STEPPING UP" Program (2 books, 4 CD's) | | * | |
| | | | | | |
| | | | | | |
| Shipping $9.95 for shipping and handling for each program ordered (in the US) | | | | | |
| Miscellaneous | | | | | |
| TAX (8.1%) (AZ. Residents only) | | | | | |
| **SUBTOTAL** | | | | | |
| **BALANCE DUE** | | | | | |

* Please call number above for current pricing

### *Thank You for your order!*